Nursery Rhymes
Itsy, Bitsy Spider
And Other Best-Loved Rhymes

ARCTURUS

ARCTURUS

This edition published in 2014 by Arcturus Publishing Limited
26/27 Bickels Yard, 151–153 Bermondsey Street,
London SE1 3HA

ISBN: 978-1-84858-770-0
CH002603US
Supplier 15, Date 0114, Print run 2983

Printed in China

Contents

Itsy, Bitsy Spider

Itsy, bitsy spider,
Went up the water spout.
Down came the rain,
And washed the spider out.

Out came the sun and
Dried up all the rain.
And itsy, bitsy spider
Went up the spout again.

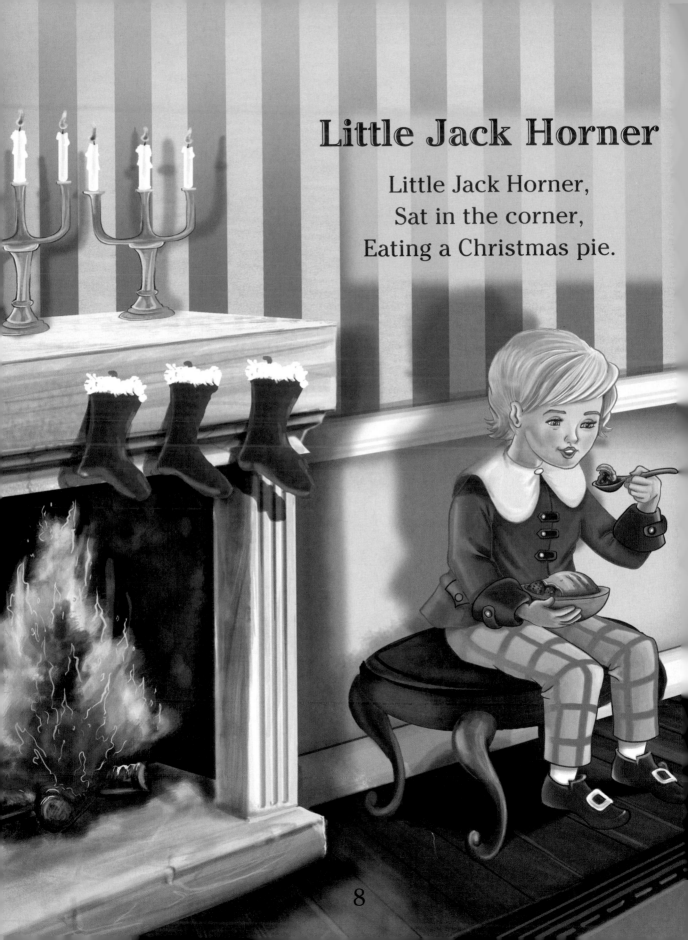

Little Jack Horner

Little Jack Horner,
Sat in the corner,
Eating a Christmas pie.

He stuck in his thumb,
And pulled out a plum,
And said, "What a good boy am I!"

The Queen of Hearts

The Queen of Hearts,
She made some tarts,
All on a summer's day.
The Knave of Hearts,
He stole the tarts,
And took them clean away.

The King of Hearts,
Called for the tarts,
And beat the Knave full sore.
The Knave of Hearts,
Brought back the tarts,
And vowed he'd steal no more.

Jack Be Nimble

Jack, be nimble,
Jack, be quick,
Jack, jump over the candlestick.

Little Boy Blue

Little Boy Blue,
Come blow your horn.
The sheep's in the meadow,
The cow's in the corn.

Where is the boy
Who looks after the sheep?
"He's under the haystack,
Fast asleep."

14

Will you wake him?
"No, not I,
For if I do,
He'll be sure to cry."

Peter, Peter, Pumpkin Eater

Peter, Peter, pumpkin eater,
Had a wife but couldn't keep her.
He put her in a pumpkin shell,
And there he kept her very well.

Peter, Peter, pumpkin eater,
Had another, but didn't love her.
Peter learned to read and spell,
And then he loved her very well.

Ring Around the Rosie

Ring around the rosie,
A pocket full of posies,
Ashes, ashes,
We all fall down.

The King has sent his daughter,
To fetch a pail of water,
Ashes, ashes,
We all fall down.

The birds upon the steeple,
Sit high above the people,
Ashes, ashes,
We all fall down.

The wedding bells are ringing,
The boys and girls are singing,
Ashes, ashes,
We all fall down.

Ladybug, Ladybug

Ladybug, ladybug, fly away home!
Your house is on fire, your children are gone.
All but one, and her name is Anne,
And she crept under the pudding pan.

Ladybug, ladybug, fly away home!
The field mouse is gone to her nest,
The daisies have shut up their sleepy red eyes,
And the bees and the birds are at rest.

Ladybug, ladybug, fly away home!
The glowworm is lighting her lamp,
The dew's falling fast, and your fine speckled wings
Will flag with the close-clinging damp.

24

Ladybug, ladybug, fly away home!
The fairy bells tinkle afar.
Make haste or they'll catch you and harness you fast
With a cobweb to Oberon's car.

Peter Piper

Peter Piper picked a peck of pickled peppers.
A peck of pickled peppers Peter Piper picked.

If Peter Piper picked a peck of pickled peppers,
Where's the peck of pickled peppers
Peter Piper picked?

What Are Little Boys Made Of?

What are little boys made of?
What are little boys made of?
Snips and snails, and puppy-dogs' tails;
That's what little boys are made of.

What are little girls made of?
What are little girls made of?
Sugar and spice, and all that's nice;
That's what little girls are made of.

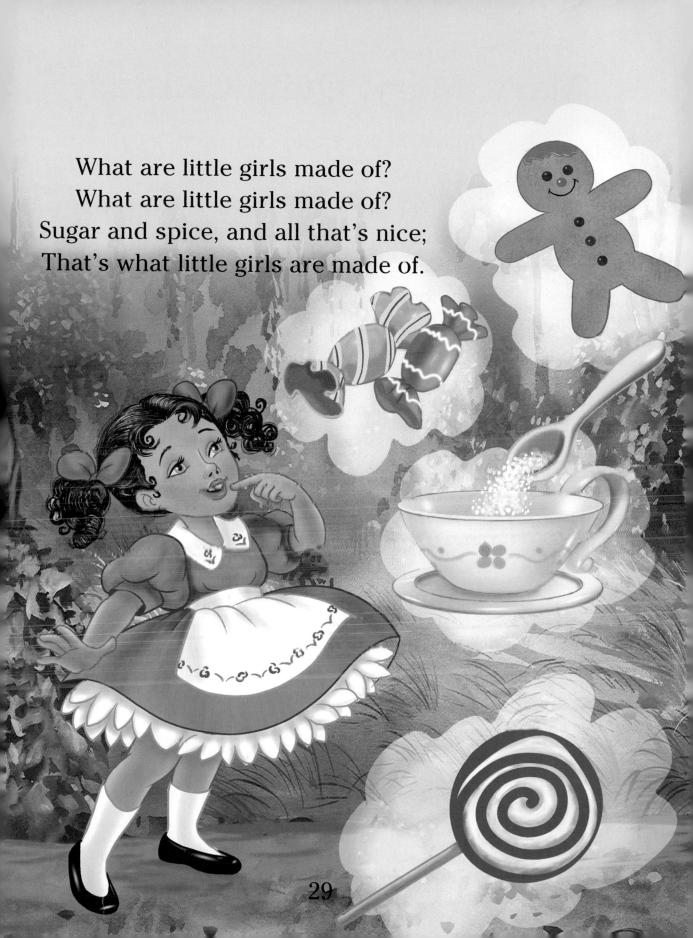

Mary, Mary, Quite Contrary

Mary, Mary, quite contrary,
How does your garden grow?
With silver bells and cockle shells,
And pretty maids all in a row.

30